THE
MICROWAVE
LIBRARY

COOKING WITH
Meat

VERONICA BULL

THE MICROWAVE LIBRARY

COOKING WITH

Meat

VERONICA BULL

NEW BURLINGTON BOOKS

THE
MICROWAVE
LIBRARY

A QUINTET BOOK

Published by New Burlington Books
6 Blundell Street
London N7 9BH

ISBN 1-85076-096-9

This book was designed and produced by
Quintet Publishing Limited
6 Blundell Street
London N7 9BH

Art Director: Peter Bridgewater
Photographers: Michael Bull and Trevor Wood
Home Economist: Veronica Bull
Typeset in Great Britain by
Central Southern Typesetters, Eastbourne
Manufactured in Hong Kong by Regent
Publishing Services Limited
Printed in Hong Kong by Leefung-Asco Printers
Limited

CONTENTS

MEAT

MEAT forms a major part of the household budget. By using the correct cooking methods your microwave oven will enable you to produce moist, tender dishes representing good value for money.

For the housewife who is concerned with healthy eating, the microwave cooking method preserves nutrients and helps to cut down the use of fats.

As with conventional cooking, prime quality meat will produce the best result. This however, does not mean the less tender cuts cannot be cooked successfully. You will achieve excellent results with curries, casseroles and stews cooked at low temperatures over a longer period. These dishes reheat in minutes, losing none of the original freshness, they remain moist and succulent with a flavour that develops and improves. For this reason they are an excellent choice when entertaining, allowing you to spend more time with your guests while producing the perfect meal.

Large roasts of meat brown naturally; smaller cuts can be browned in a browning dish, or by conventional means before or after the cooking period. If a crisp finish is not essential, a sauce or glaze will improve the appearance of the dish.

The recipes featured in this book include exotic dishes such as Chinese Pancakes and Tandoori Chicken, together with a selection of more traditional fare. Different cooking methods have been included to show that with colourful ingredients and garnishes. Microwaved meat offers a tasty and attractive selection of dishes that will make every meal a special occasion.

Veronica L. Bull

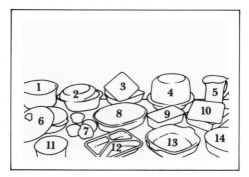

A selection of cookware, some of it specially designed for the microwave oven, which is suitable for microwaving.

1 Thorpak cake dish **2** Thorpak casserole dish **3** Microware freezer dishes **4** Roasting dish **5** Thorpak jug **6** Browning dish **7** Minidishes (ramekins) **8** Double microwave serving dish **9** Glass loaf pan **10** Glass casserole with lid **11** Cake or soufflé dish **12** Three-section vegetable dish **13** Browning dish **14** Glass ovenproof dish

ABOUT THE MICROWAVE OVEN

IF YOU are new to cooking with the microwave, the first thing to do is to read the instruction booklet supplied with your model. This will tell you all you need to know about how your cooker works and how to operate it.

Microwave cookers work by emitting concentrated infra red radiation that penetrates and therefore heats food much faster than conventional cookers. They consequently save considerably on cooking time.

The microwave is like any other kitchen appliance that makes life easier for the cook. Once you are used to it, which takes remarkably little time for such a sophisticated gadget, experience will tell you how long it will take to cook or reheat a given dish. If in doubt, always undercook – you can easily add on another minute or so.

To familiarize yourself with the cooker try baking a potato. Scrub the potato and prick the skin a few times with a fork. Lay it on a piece of absorbent kitchen paper and cook on full power for about 6 minutes for a 175 g/6 oz potato. Stop cooking half-way through to turn the potato over. A successfully baked potato will demonstrate how easy microwave cooking is.

Remember to stir or rearrange items during cooking or the food may not be evenly cooked, and

always cover a dish with a lid or cling film (plastic wrap) which you have pierced in two or three places with a knife to make vents through which the steam can escape.

Don't use anything metallic in the microwave, and this includes china decorated with silver or gold leaf. If you want to test if a dish is microwave-proof, put it in the oven next to a cup of water and cook on full for a minute. If the water is hot and the dish stays cool, it is safe to use. If the dish is hotter than the water, avoid using it.

Always prick the skins of vegetables and fish to prevent them from bursting. Eggs should always be pricked for the same reason. Never put an egg in its shell in the microwave – it will explode.

All the recipes in this book are timed for a 700-watt oven, and where the recipe times are not specific, this is to avoid errors. A microwave may be a scientific instrument, but even identical ovens may cook at slightly different rates, and neither cooks nor food can be standardized – no two carrots are the same shape and no two cooks cut them in the same way.

However, the following can be taken as a general guide for ovens with a different power rating from that of the model used in the book. For every minute of cooking time specified in these recipes, add 5 seconds for a 650-watt oven, 10 seconds for a 600-watt oven and 30 seconds for a 500-watt oven. But remember, it is *always* safer to undercook and test.

Crockery, cutlery (flatware, glassware and cookware such as this must NOT be used in a microwave oven.

1 Ceramics with metal decoration **2** Dishes with metal decoration and glazes containing metal **3** Cutlery (silverware or flatware) **4** Metal flan tin and disposable foil bakeware **5** Glassware with metal rim or bands **6** Metal pots and pans **7** Metal bakeware **8** Metal skewers or fondue forks

HAMBURGERS

SERVES 4–6 / SET: HIGH

Ingredients

1 onion, finely chopped
1/4 cup/50 g/2 oz breadcrumbs
1 egg, beaten
500 g/1 lb 2 oz Savoury Hamburger Mixture (page 11)
4–6 hamburger buns
GARNISH
sliced tomatoes
onion
lettuce leaves
relish of your choice

◆ Add the onions, breadcrumbs and egg to the Mixture and combine well.

◆ Divide into 4 or 6 even portions and shape into patties.

◆ Heat a browning dish to the maximum recommended by the manufacturer and press the hamburgers onto the bottom. Cook for 7½–9 minutes, turning the hamburgers over after 4 minutes.

◆ If you prefer, cook for only half the above time and finish off under the grill or on a barbecue.

◆ Serve with onion, tomato, lettuce and relish in a hot or cold bun.

Hamburgers

SAVOURY HAMBURGER MIXTURE

SERVES 4 / SET: HIGH

Ingredients

450 g/1 lb minced (ground) beef
30 ml/2 tbsp tomato ketchup
60 ml/4 tbsp soya sauce
30 ml/2 tbsp chopped fresh herbs
2.5 ml/½ tbsp celery salt
15 ml/1 tbsp horseradish sauce
15 ml/1 tbsp French mustard

◆ Combine all the ingredients in a large bowl and mix well. Place 1 tbsp on a plate and cook on high for 2 minutes. Taste to test for flavour.

◆ This is the basic, uncooked recipe to which sauces and liquids may be added for 'wet' dishes or eggs and breadcrumbs for 'dry' dishes such as hamburgers, meatballs etc.

◆ To cook this dish on its own, place the mixture in a casserole dish, cover and cook for 7–9 minutes, stirring twice during the cooking time. Add sauce or gravy as required.

LEEKS AU GRATIN

*SERVES 2—4 / SET: HIGH
AND MEDIUM*

Ingredients

*350 g/12 oz Savoury Hamburger Mixture
(page 11)*

6 tbsp/75 ml/3 fl oz hot thick gravy

4 large leeks

¼ cup/50 ml/2 fl oz water

100 g/4 oz grated cheese

◆ Place the mince (ground beef) in a
dish, cover and cook on high for 6—7
minutes. Stir after 3 minutes. Drain
off any fat, then add the gravy and stir
well. Keep to one side.

◆ Trim the leeks, and with a sharp
knife slice down the length, cutting
only as deep as the centre. Spread the
leaves apart and wash. Select the
widest leaves and place in a dish with
the water, cover and cook on high for
1½—2 minutes until softened. Pour
over cold water, drain and pat dry
with absorbent paper.

◆ Lay the leeks flat and place approx
15 ml/1 tbsp of mince mixture at the
narrow end of each leaf. Roll up to
enclose the meat. Place in a dish, cover
and cook on high for 4—5 minutes or
until heated through. Sprinkle over
the grated cheese and cook,
uncovered, on high for 2 minutes.

STUFFED CANNELLONI IN TOMATO SAUCE

SERVES 2 / SET: HIGH

Ingredients

8 cannelloni tubes
5 ml/1 tsp dried oregano
1 clove of garlic, crushed
30 ml/2 tbsp tomato purée (paste)
450 g/1 lb Savoury Hamburger Mixture (page 11)

SAUCE

1 small onion, peeled and finely chopped
1 clove garlic, peeled and crushed
5 ml/1 tsp dried oregano
2 tbsp/25 g/1 oz butter, diced
2 tbsp/25 g/1 oz plain flour
400 g/14 oz can of tomatoes, chopped
60 ml/4 tbsp tomato purée (paste)
45 ml/3 tbsp garlic vinegar
15 ml/1 tbsp sugar
salt and pepper
4 slices of mozzarella cheese

◆ Stir the garlic, oregano and 2 tbsp of tomato purée (paste) into the meat mixture. Place in a shallow dish and cook for 3 minutes, stirring halfway through the cooking time. At this stage the meat will not be completely cooked.

◆ For the sauce, place the onion, garlic, oregano and butter in a bowl, cover and cook for 3 minutes. Stir in the flour, tomatoes, vinegar, sugar and tomato purée (paste) with the salt and pepper (to taste). Cook uncovered for 4–5 minutes. Dilute with a little water or red wine if the sauce is too thick.

◆ Stuff the cannelloni tubes with the meat mixture. Place them in an oblong dish, pour on the sauce, cover and cook for 12–15 minutes. Place the cheese slices on top of the cannelloni and melt for 2 minutes or brown under a conventional grill (broiler).

Stuffed cannelloni in tomato sauce

LASAGNE

SERVES 4—6 / SET: HIGH

Ingredients

175 g/6 oz lasagne
7 ml/½ tsp oil
3¾ cups/900 ml/1½ pts boiling water
salt to taste
500 g/1 lb 2 oz Savoury Hamburger Mixture (page 11)
400 g/15 oz can of tomatoes, chopped
225 g/8 oz sliced button mushrooms
1 clove garlic, crushed
175 g/6 oz blue cheese
150 ml/5 oz single (light) cream
mushroom slices to garnish

◆ Place the lasagne in a deep dish, cover with the boiling water, add oil and salt. Cover and cook for 9–11 minutes. Set aside covered. Alternatively cook on a conventional hob (burner) according to the instructions on the package while you prepare the remainder of the dish.

◆ Place the beef mixture in a large shallow dish, cover and cook for 5 minutes. Drain, add the tomatoes, garlic and mushrooms, stir well and cook for 5 minutes, stirring occasionally.

◆ Drain the pasta and, in a shallow oblong dish, place alternative layers of meat and lasagne, finishing with a layer of lasagne.

◆ Place the gorgonzola in a bowl and cook for 1 minute. Mash it and blend in the cream. Replace in the oven and cook for a further minute. Blend to a smooth sauce and add it to the dish. Brown under a conventional grill (broiler).

◆ Cook the mushroom slices with a little butter for 1 minute and use as a garnish.

MEAT LOAF

SERVES 4—6 / SET: HIGH

Ingredients

225 g/8 oz Savoury Hamburger Mixture (page 11)

225 g/8 oz pork sausage meat

1 medium onion, peeled and finely chopped

1 clove garlic, peeled and crushed

2 cups/100 g/4 oz breadcrumbs

1 egg, beaten

salt and pepper to taste

◆ Place the butter, onion and garlic in a bowl. Cover and cook for 2 minutes.

◆ Mix together the beef, pork, breadcrumbs and seasoning to taste. Stir in the onion, garlic and beaten egg. Combine well and cook uncovered for 5 minutes. Stir and break up with a fork.

◆ Transfer to a microwave loaf dish or any other suitable container, press down and smooth the top. Cook for 5–7 minutes.

◆ Chill and turn out. Slice and serve with salad.

BRAISED BEEF

SERVES 4 / SET: HIGH & LOW

Ingredients

675 g/1½ lb braising steak (chuck, skirt, flank), cubed

1 large onion, chopped

3 medium sized carrots, sliced

225 g/8 oz button mushrooms

1 celery stick, sliced

30 ml/2 tbsp tomato purée (paste)

5 ml/1 tsp mixed dried herbs

25 g/1 oz butter, diced

25 g/1 oz plain flour

2 cups/450 ml/¾ pint hot beef stock (broth)

◆ Place the onions, carrots and celery in a large dish with 2 tbsp of stock. Cover and cook on high for 5–6 minutes.

◆ Stir in the meat and butter, cover and cook on high for 4 minutes. Add the flour, mushrooms, herbs, tomato purée (paste) and beef stock (broth). Stir, cover and cook on high for 6–7 minutes.

◆ Cook for a further 40 minutes on low. Stir several times during the cooking period.

◆ Let it stand covered for 10 minutes. Garnish with parsley and serve.

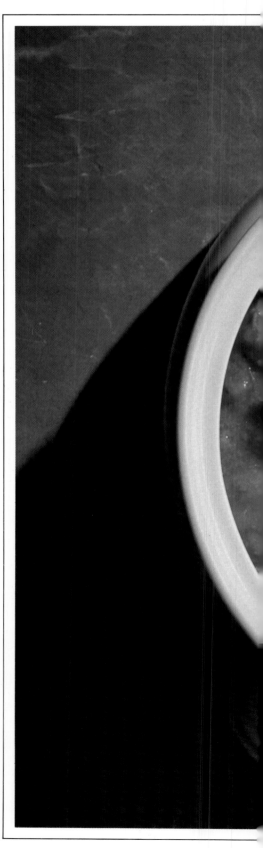

Braised beef

CREOLE STEAK

SERVES 4 / SET: HIGH

Ingredients

4 fillet steaks, approx 200 g/6–7 oz each
¼ cup/50 g/2 oz butter, diced
2 onions, finely chopped
4 celery sticks, sliced
100 g/4 oz button mushrooms, chopped
400 g/14 oz can of tomatoes, finely chopped
30 ml/2 tbsp tomato purée (paste)
15 ml/1 tbsp soy sauce
salt and pepper to taste

◆ Place the steaks in a casserole dish. Cook uncovered for 3–4 minutes depending on how rare you like your steak. Turn over and rearrange halfway through the cooking time.

◆ Place the butter, onions, celery and mushrooms in a dish, cover and cook for 6 minutes, stirring after 3 minutes.

◆ Stir in the remaining ingredients, season to taste, cover and cook for 4 minutes.

◆ Arrange the steaks on a serving dish, pour over the sauce and sprinkle with parsley.

Creole Steak

BEEF GOULASH

SERVES 4 / SET: FULL AND MEDIUM

Ingredients

5½ cups/1 kg/2 lb lean braising steak
½ cup/2 oz/50 g flour
½ tbs paprika
2 tbs oil
2 cloves garlic, crushed
1 tbs tomato paste
2 onions sliced
2½ cups/600 ml/1 pint hot beef stock
1 bayleaf
200 g/7 oz can tomatoes, mashed
4 tbs yoghurt
2 tbs parsley, chopped

◆ Cut the meat into bite-sized cubes. Mix the flour and paprika together and toss the meat in the mixture.

◆ Heat a browning dish on full power according to manufacturer's instructions. Pour the oil into the dish and cook on full for 1 minute. Add the beef and cook for 5 minutes on full, turning frequently to brown all sides.

◆ Place the meat in a casserole with garlic, tomato paste, onion, stock, bayleaf and tomatoes. Cover and cook on full for 45 minutes until beef is tender. Leave to stand for 5 minutes.

◆ Spoon the yoghurt over the casserole and serve garnished with parsley. The dish goes well with noodles or mashed potatoes.

SAUSAGE CASSEROLE WITH DUMPLINGS

SERVES 4 / SET: HIGH AND MEDIUM

Ingredients

15 ml/1 tbsp cooking oil
1 medium onion, chopped
2 rashers (slices) (lean or Canadian) bacon, diced
8 sausages (links)
550 ml/1 pt hot gravy
100 g/4 oz button mushrooms
100 g/4 oz mixed frozen vegetables, defrosted

DUMPLINGS

4 tbsp/50 g/2 oz self-raising (self-rising) flour
2 tbsp/25 g/1 oz beef suet or shortening
pinch dried sage
salt and pepper to taste
water

◆ For the dumplings, mix together all the ingredients, add enough water to make a soft dough, then on a floured board form the dough into four dumplings. Set to one side.

◆ Preheat a browning dish to maximum as recommended by the manufacturer. Add the butter, onions, sausages and bacon. Cover and cook on high for 7 minutes, stirring once. Add the gravy, mushrooms and vegetables, cover and cook on medium for 6–7 minutes. Then add the dumplings, cook on high for 2 minutes and serve.

Liver sausage casserole with dumplings

BRAISED TOPSIDE (TOP ROUND)

SERVES 6—8 / SET: MEDIUM AND LOW

Ingredients

1.4—1.8 kg/3—4 lb topside (top round) of beef
1 beef stock cube
1/2 cup/125 ml/4 fl oz hot water
15 ml/1 tbsp Worcestershire sauce
2 bay leaves
1 large carrot, sliced
2 celery sticks, sliced
1 onion, quartered

◆ Trim off excess fat, pierce the meat all over with a skewer and place in a casserole dish.

◆ Dissolve the stock cube in the hot water and Worcestershire sauce and add to the dish. Cover and cook on medium for 35 minutes.

◆ Turn the meat and add the vegetables and bay leaves, cover and cook on low for 70 minutes. Leave it standing, covered, for 10 minutes. If using a microwave thermometer, remove it from the oven when the temperature reaches 65°C/150°F.

BEEF AND BACON CASEROLE

SERVES 4 / SET: HIGH AND MEDIUM

Ingredients

1 tbsp/25 g/1 oz butter

300 g/12 oz beef, cut into strips

3 rashers (slices) of bacon without rind, chopped

1 large onion, quartered and finely sliced

3 medium carrots, thinly sliced

2 cups/400 ml/15 fl oz hot chicken stock

2.5 ml/½ tsp dried basil

2 tbsp/25 g/1 oz flour for coating

◆ Toss the liver in flour to coat. Preheat a browning dish to maximum, according to the manufacturer's instructions. Add the butter, liver, bacon, onions and carrots. Cover and cook on high for 8 minutes, stirring once.

◆ Add the stock and herbs. Cook on medium for 8–10 minutes.

LAMB HOTPOT

SERVES 4 / SET: HIGH AND LOW

Ingredients

570 g/1¼ lb lamb steaks, cut from the leg

2 tbsp/25 g/1 oz flour

¼ cup/50 g/2 oz butter, diced

1 onion, finely sliced

1 clove garlic, crushed

1 leek, trimmed and sliced

2 large carrots, finely sliced

4 celery sticks, sliced

1 bay leaf

1 chicken stock cube, crumbled

30 ml/2 tbsp tomato purée (paste)

400 g/14 oz can of tomatoes

100 g/4 oz button mushrooms

salt and pepper to taste

2 large cooked potatoes, sliced

◆ Place 1 tbsp/25 g/1 oz butter in a large deep casserole dish. Cook on high for 1 minute then add the onion, garlic and leek. Cover and cook on high for 3 minutes. Add the carrots, celery and 30 ml/2 tbsp of juice from the tomatoes. Cover and cook on high for 6 minutes.

◆ Trim the fat from the lamb and cut it into cubes. Toss the cubes in the flour and add to the vegetables together with the tinned tomatoes, stock cube, tomato purée (paste) and bay leaf. Cover and cook on high for 6 minutes, stirring halfway through the cooking time.

◆ Add the mushrooms, reduce to low and cook for a further 30 minutes, stirring every 5 minutes.

◆ Taste and season the stew, then layer the potatoes over the meat, dot with butter and brown in a conventional oven.

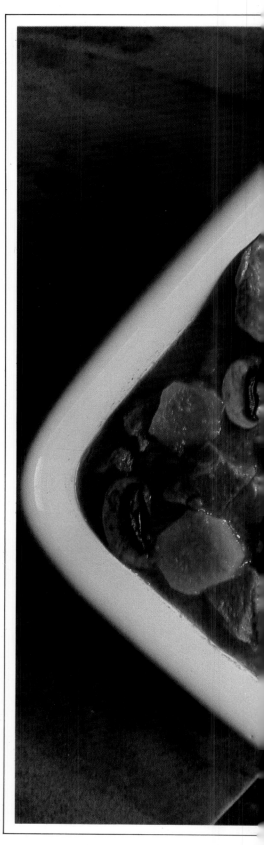

Lamb hotpot

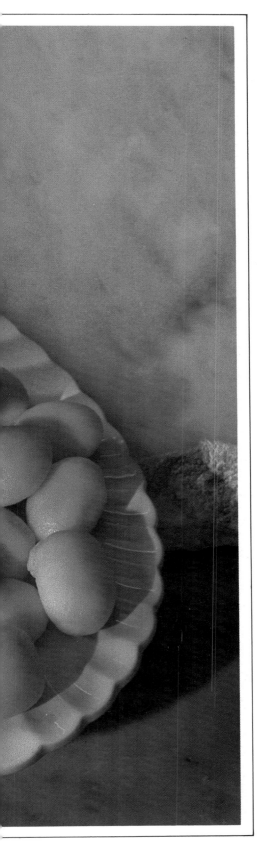

Guard of honor

GUARD OF HONOUR

SERVES 4 / SET: HIGH AND MEDIUM

Ingredients

2 pieces best end of neck (rib chops left in 1 piece), 5–6 cutlets (chops) (approx 1 kg/ 2 lb) each

30 ml/2 tbsp cranberry sauce

15 ml/1 tbsp mint jelly

cutlet frills (optional)

◆ Weigh the meat and calculate cooking time at 2 minutes per 450 g/ 1 lb on high initially, plus 7–9 minutes per 450 g/1 lb on medium.

◆ Score the fatty side of each piece of meat, interlock the trimmed bone ends to form a 'guard of honour', meaty side inwards. Wrap a piece of foil around each bone end to prevent burning.

◆ Place the cranberry and mint jelly in a bowl and melt them for 1–2 minutes on high. Paint the fatty sides of the lamb mixture. Place the lamb on a roasting rack, cover and cook on high for 4 minutes. Reduce to medium and cook for 15–16 minutes. Remove the lid for the last 8 minutes. Paint on more cranberry mixture. Loosely wrap with foil and leave it to stand for 10 minutes.

◆ Replace the foil on the bone ends with the paper frills (if used) and set on a serving dish with vegetables.

◆ Variation: Stuff the lamb with your favourite stuffing (dressing) mix (as you would a crown roast) and allow an extra 3 minutes on the cooking time.

SAGE AND MOZZARELLA-STUFFED CHICKEN

SERVES 4 / SET: FULL

Ingredients

1.5–2 kg/3½–4 lb oven ready chicken

6 sage leaves

¼–½ cup/25–50 g/1–2 oz mozzarella cheese, sliced

2 tbs/25 g/1 oz butter

1 onion, chopped

1 cup/50 g/2 oz white breadcrumbs

2 tsp fresh sage, chopped

salt-freshly ground black pepper

⅝ cup/150 ml/¼ pint hot chicken stock

2 tbs/25 g/1 oz butter

1 tbs brown sugar

1 tbs sherry

◆ Grasp the flap of skin at the end of the bird and with the other hand, pull the skin away from the flesh as far as you can. Slide in the sage leaves and cheese slices.

◆ Place the butter and onion in a bowl, cover and cook for 3 minutes. Mix in the breadcrumbs, sage, seasoning and stock to form a moist, doughy consistency. Stuff the chicken and cook 8–10 minutes per 450 g/1 lb.

◆ Halfway through the cooking time, place the butter, sugar and sherry in a small jug. Cook for 1 minute. Remove the bird from the oven and brush with the glaze. Return bird to oven, giving the dish a half turn, and complete cooking. Check to see if the chicken is done by sticking a skewer into it where the leg joins with the breast. The juices should run out clear.

◆ Allow to stand for 15 minutes before serving.

THE
MICROWAVE
LIBRARY

MEAT

LAMB CHOPS AND CRANBERRY JELLY

SERVES 2 / SET: HIGH AND MEDIUM

Ingredients

4 noisettes of lamb, each 75 g/3 oz, 2.5 cm/1 inch thick

400 g/14 oz can of consommé

15 ml/1 tbsp gelatine

90 ml/6 tbsp cranberry jelly

5 ml/1 tsp fresh or 2.5 ml/½ tsp dried mint

mint sprigs to garnish

◆ Arrange the chops in a shallow dish. Cook on high for 2 minutes, rearrange, and cook for a further 2 minutes. Cover and set aside.

◆ Place the consommé, cranberry jelly and herbs in a bowl and cook on high for 3 minutes. Do not allow it to boil. Sprinkle on the gelatine and stir until dissolved.

◆ Remove chops from the dish and arrange on a serving plate. Brush with the stock and chill.

◆ Pour the consommé into a shallow dish and chill until jellied. Chop roughly and arrange around the chops. Garnish with sprigs of mint and serve with salad.

Lamp chops & cranberry jelly

LAMB AND MUSHROOM RISOTTO

SERVES 2 / SET: HIGH

Ingredients

225 g/8 oz cooked lamb, cubed

2 tbsp/25 g/1 oz butter

⅔ cup/100 g/4 oz long grain rice

5 ml/1 tsp garam masala (available at Indian groceries) or curry powder

5 ml/1 tsp curry powder

2 cups/400 ml/15 fl oz chicken stock, made with a cube

100 g/4 oz button mushrooms

1 small onion, finely chopped

100 g/4 oz mixed frozen vegetables

◆ Place the butter in a large deep dish, cook for 1 minute, add the onion, cover and cook for 1½ minutes.

◆ Stir in the rice, garam masala and curry powder. Pour on the stock and cook, covered, for 10 minutes.

◆ Stir in the remaining ingredients. Cook for 5 minutes or until the rice is tender but firm. Allow the dish to stand for 5 minutes.

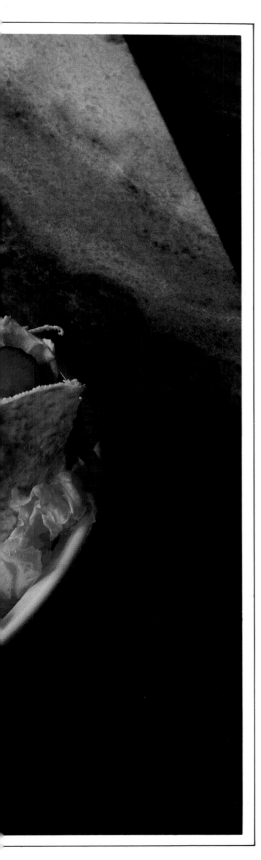

PITA POCKETS

*SERVES 4 / SET: LOW,
MEDIUM AND HIGH*

Ingredients

454 g/1 lb lamb fillet, cubed
1 tbsp/14 g/½ oz butter
30 ml/2 tbsp soy sauce
30 ml/2 tbsp lemon juice
15 ml/1 tbsp honey
4 pitta breads
30 ml/2 tbsp mayonnaise
12 cucumber slices
12 tomato slices
1 lettuce heart
1 small onion, cut into rings

◆ Mix together the soy sauce, lemon juice and honey. Add the meat cubes and marinate for at least 2 hours.

◆ Heat a browning dish to maximum, according to the manufacturer's instructions. Remove the meat from the marinade, add butter to the browning dish and stir in the meat. Cook on high for 2 minutes, reduce to medium and cook for a further 9 minutes. Cover and reserve.

◆ Place the pita breads on 2 layers of kitchen paper and warm on low for 2 minutes. Remove from the oven, cut in half, open up the 'pocket' and spread the inside with mayonnaise. Shred the lettuce and add a little to each pocket with a few slices of tomato, cucumber and onion. Pile in the lamb. Alternatively, skewer meat and vegetables on wooden kebab sticks and serve with the pita bread and rice.

Pita pockets

LAMB CASSEROLE

*SERVES 4 / SET: HIGH
AND MEDIUM*

Ingredients

750 g/1½ lb boned shoulder of lamb, cubed
1 tbsp/15 g/½ oz flour
1 tbsp/15 g/½ oz butter
2 medium onions, sliced
1 large apple, sliced
100 g/4 oz stoned (pitted) prunes
½ cup/150 ml/5 fl oz chicken stock made with a cube
½ cup/150 ml/5 fl oz red wine
salt and pepper to taste

◆ Toss the lamb in the flour to coat. Place the butter in a casserole dish and cook on high for 1 minute. Add the onions, cover and cook on high for 2 minutes. Add the lamb and cook on high for 5 minutes.

◆ Stir in the apple, prunes, chicken stock and red wine. Cover and cook on medium for 25–30 minutes. Stir twice during the cooking period. Season to taste and serve.

ARMENIAN LAMB WITH PILAFF

SERVES 4 / SET: FULL

Ingredients

1 kg/2 lb fillet end leg of lamb
1 tbs oil
2 tbs/25 g/1 oz butter
2 onions, chopped
1 clove garlic, chopped
4 tbs/25 g/1 oz flour
1 tsp ground cumin
1/2 tsp ground allspice
2 tbs tomato paste
5/8 cup/300 ml/1/2 pint hot chicken stock
salt/freshly ground black pepper

PILAFF

3 tbs/40 g/1 1/2 oz butter
1 small onion, chopped
1 cup/250 g/8 oz long-grain rice
1 7/8 cups/450 ml/3/4 pint hot chicken stock
salt/freshly ground black pepper
1/2 cup/75 g/3 oz currants
1/2 cup/75 g/3 oz almonds, blanched and chopped

◆ Remove meat from bone and cut into bite-sized cubes.

◆ Pour oil into a bowl, add butter and cook for 1 minute. Stir in onion and garlic and cook for 3 minutes. Add the meat and cook, covered, for 3 minutes.

◆ Stir in the flour and add remaining ingredients. Cook, covered, for 10 minutes. Allow to stand for 15 minutes then cook for a further 6 minutes.

◆ To make the pilaff, place the butter in a large shallow dish and cook for 1 minute. Stir in onion and rice and cook for 4 minutes.

◆ Add stock and seasoning and cook for 15 minutes or until rice is fluffy, adding extra stock if necessary. Check seasoning and stir in currants and almonds before serving with the lamb.

Armenian Lamb with Pilaff

KOFTA MEAT BALLS

SERVES 2 / SET: HIGH

Ingredients

450 g/1 lb minced (ground) lamb

2.5 ml/½ tsp garam masala (available at Indian groceries) or curry powder

2.5 ml/½ tsp ground ginger

2 cloves garlic, crushed

2.5 ml/½ tsp ground cumin

1 egg

salt to taste

15 ml/1 tbsp vegetable oil

◆ Mix together all the ingredients except the oil and roll into small balls.

◆ Meanwhile, preheat a browning dish to maximum as recommended by the manufacturer. Add the oil 30 seconds before the end of this time.

◆ Quickly add the meatballs and cook for 5 minutes, turning once during the cooking time.

MOUSSAKA

SERVES 4 / SET: HIGH

Ingredients

450 g/1 lb minced (ground) lamb
2 tbsp/25 g/1 oz butter
1 large onion, finely sliced
4 medium aubergines (eggplants)
1 beef stock cube dissolved in 45 ml/ 3 tbsp water
60 ml/4 tbsp tomato purée (paste)
salt and pepper to taste

SAUCE

2 tbsp/25 g/1 oz butter
2 tbsp/25 g/1 oz flour
1¼ cups/285 ml/10 fl oz milk
1½ cups/150 g/6 oz grated (shredded) cheese

◆ Thinly slice the aubergines (eggplants), sprinkle with salt and leave for 15 minutes. Pour off the bitter juices, rinse and drain.

◆ Meanwhile, place the butter in a dish, cook for 1 minute. Stir in the onions and aubergines when they are ready and cook covered for 5–6 minutes. Add the meat, stock and tomato purée. Cook covered for 5 minutes.

◆ To make the sauce, cook the butter for 1 minute, add the flour and cook for 2 minutes. Stir in the milk and cook for 3 minutes, stirring every minute until thickened. Add the cheese, stir and keep to one side.

◆ Place half of the meat mixture in a deep casserole, top with half the sauce, then the remaining meat and finally the remainder of the sauce.

◆ Place the dish in the oven and cook for 10 minutes.

◆ Brown under a preheated conventional grill (broiler) and serve.

LAMB CURRY

SERVES 4 / SET: HIGH & LOW

Ingredients

1 kg/2 lb 3 oz shoulder of lamb, cubed
2 tbsp/25 g/1 oz butter
4 cloves garlic, peeled and crushed
1 medium onion, finely sliced
15 g/½ oz freshly grated ginger root
2.5 ml/½ tsp ground mustard seed
2.5 ml/½ tsp ground fenugreek
2.5 ml/½ tsp ground cumin
2.5 ml/½ tsp turmeric
5 ml/1 tsp chilli powder
400 g/14 oz can tomatoes, finely chopped
60 ml/2 fl oz white wine vinegar
15 ml/1 tbsp sugar

◆ Place half the butter in a dish and cook on high for 1 minute. Add the garlic and onion, cook on high, covered, for 1½ minutes. Add the grated ginger, ground mustard seed, fenugreek, cumin, turmeric and chilli powder and cook for a further 1½ minutes on high. Stir in the tomatoes, vinegar and sugar. Place to one side.

◆ Preheat a browning dish to maximum, according to the manufacturer's instructions. Add the remaining butter and meat and cook on high for 4 minutes, stirring once halfway through the cooking time. Add the curry sauce, cover and cook on low for 25 minutes. Stir every 10 minutes. Let it stand for 5 minutes.

◆ Serve with plain boiled rice.

Lamb curry

PORK SPARE RIBS IN BARBECUE SAUCE

SERVES 2 / SET: HIGH AND LOW

Ingredients

6 meaty pork spare ribs, total weight approx 675 g/1½ lb
1 small onion, finely sliced
1 tbsp/15 g/½ oz butter
SAUCE
30 ml/2 tbsp honey
30 ml/2 tbsp soya sauce
60 ml/4 tbsp tomato ketchup
15 ml/1 tbsp white wine vinegar
spring onions (scallions) to garnish

◆ Place the butter and onion in a shallow casserole. Cover and cook on high for 3 minutes.

◆ Add the ribs to the casserole dish and pour over the sauce, turning the ribs to coat. Cook on high for 4 minutes.

◆ Spoon over the sauce again, cover and cook on low for 25 minutes, rearranging and turning the ribs every 5 minutes. Drain the sauce into a saucepan and boil on the stove top until reduced and of a syrupy consistency, about 10 minutes.

◆ Place the ribs on a serving dish, coat with the sauce and garnish with spring onions (scallions).

◆ Serve with rice or baked potatoes and salad.

SWEET AND SOUR PORK

SERVES 4 / SET: HIGH AND MEDIUM

Ingredients

450 g/1 lb pork fillet, cut into strips
60 ml/4 tbsp soy sauce
60 ml/4 tbsp dry sherry
15 ml/1 tbsp sesame oil
1/2 small yellow (bell) pepper
1/2 small (chili) red pepper
1 medium carrot
2 tsp cornflour dissolved in a little water
2 pineapple rings to garnish
2 spring onions (scallions)

SAUCE

30 ml/2 tbsp vinegar
60 ml/4 tbsp tomato ketchup
60 ml/4 tbsp honey
120 ml/8 tbsp pineapple juice

◆ Marinate the pork strips in the soy sauce and sherry for 1 hour. Cut the (bell and chili) peppers and carrots into julienne strips.

◆ Drain the meat and heat a browning dish to the maximum recommended by the manufacturer. Add the oil and quickly toss the pork strips in the oil. Cover and cook on high for 3 minutes, stirring after 2 minutes. Drain.

◆ Add the vegetables and sauce ingredients, cover and cook on medium for 2 minutes. The vegetables should be crisp. Add the cornflour and water to the dish and cook on high for 1 minute. Stir well.

◆ Serve with plain boiled rice and garnish with pineapple rings and spring onions (scallions).

TANDOORI PORK CHIPOLATAS (LINKS)

SERVES 4 / SET: MEDIUM

Ingredients

450 g/1 lb pork chipolata sausages (links)
60 ml/4 tbsp tandoori or curry paste
30 ml/2 tbsp cooking oil

◆ Prick the sausages. Combine the tandoori or curry paste and cooking oil and marinate the sausages in the mixture for 1 hour.

◆ Preheat a browning dish to the maximum recommended by the manufacturer. Remove the chipolatas from the marinade and place them in the browning dish. Cook for 3 minutes then turn and cook for a further 4 minutes.

◆ Serve hot or cold as a snack.

Sweet & sour pork

PORK KEBABS WITH PEANUT SAUCE

SERVES 4 / SET: HIGH

Ingredients

675 g/1½ lb pork fillet, cut into 2.5 cm/1 inch cubes
1 red (sweet) pepper, coarsely chopped
1 yellow (sweet) pepper, coarsely chopped
1 small onion, quartered and layers separated
2 tbsp/25 g/1 oz butter
SAUCE
110 g/4 oz roasted peanuts, ground
30 ml/2 tbsp soya sauce
15 ml/1 tbsp sesame oil

◆ Combine the sauce ingredients and cook covered for 1½ minutes.

◆ Skewer the meat and vegetables onto wooden kebab sticks and brush with the peanut sauce.

◆ Place the kebabs on a plate in a single layer, dot with butter, cover and cook for 4 minutes. Turn and cook for a further 4 minutes.

◆ Serve with extra sauce, plain boiled rice and salad.

CHINESE PANCAKES

SERVES 4 / SET: HIGH

Ingredients

PANCAKES / MAKES 8

100 g/4 oz plain flour

1 egg

1¼ cups/300 ml/½ pint milk

pinch salt

cooking fat (shortening) to grease pan

FILLING

150 g/6 oz pork fillet, thinly sliced into strips

1 tbsp/15 g/½ oz butter

1 bunch spring onions (scallions), sliced

225 g/8 oz can of water chestnuts, thinly sliced

60 ml/4 tbsp soy sauce

30 ml/2 tbsp dry sherry

100 g/4 oz roasted salted cashew nuts

2 spring onions (scallions), to garnish

½ (sweet) red pepper – to garnish

◆ To make the pancakes, sift the flour and salt into a bowl. Make a well in the centre. Beat the egg and add it to the flour. Pour in half the milk and mix to a smooth batter. Add the remaining milk and allow to stand for 1 hour.

Melt a little fat in a frying-pan (skillet), add sufficient batter to cover the bottom of the pan thinly and cook on a conventional hob for 1 minute. Turn the pancake over and cook until golden brown. Cover and keep warm. Repeat with the remaining batter.

◆ To make the filling, heat a browning dish to maximum according to the manufacturer's instructions. Add the butter and the pork strips and cook, uncovered, for 3 minutes, stirring once. Add all the remaining ingredients and mix. Cover and cook 4 minutes.

◆ Fold the pancakes in half, then in half again. Open out the edges to make a pocket and stuff with filling.

◆ Arrange on a warmed serving dish, garnish with spring onion (scallion) tassels and julienne strips of red pepper.

CURRIED PORK SLICES

SERVES 4 / SET: HIGH

Ingredients

4 pork slices, 1 cm/½ inch thick

60 ml/4 tbsp curry paste

30 ml/2 tbsp sesame oil

◆ Mix the oil and curry paste together, add the pork slices and coat with the paste. Marinate for 30 minutes.

◆ Heat a browning dish to maximum according to the manufacturer's instructions. Add the slices, cover and cook for 4 minutes. Turn the meat over and cook for a further 4 minutes. Let them stand for 3 minutes.

◆ Serve with baked potatoes and salad.

Chinese pancakes

QUICK COOK'S PÂTÉ

S E R V E S   4   /   S E T :   H I G H

Ingredients

3 rashers (slices) of streaky (fat) bacon
1 small onion, finely chopped
1 clove garlic, crushed
5 ml/1 tsp dried sage
225 g/8 oz pig's liver, chopped
2 tbsp/25 g/1 oz butter
30 ml/2 tbsp single (light) cream
salt and pepper to taste

◆ Place the bacon, onion, garlic and herbs in a dish and cover with cling film (plastic wrap). Cook on high for 6½ minutes.

◆ Stir in the liver and butter, cover and cook on high for 6½ minutes. Let it stand for 5 minutes.

◆ Stir in the cream and purée the mixture in a blender until smooth. Season to taste.

◆ Turn into a dish, smooth the top and chill until set.

◆ Serve with hot crusty bread or triangles of toast.

STUFFED PORK CHOPS

SERVES 4 / SET: HIGH AND MEDIUM

Ingredients

4 loin pork chops, 2.5 cm/1 inch thick, 150 g/6 oz each

1 cup/100 g/4 oz grated (shredded) Cheddar cheese

STUFFING

3 tbsp/15 g/1½ oz butter

1 small onion, finely sliced

50 g/2 oz finely chopped button mushrooms

2 tbsp/50 g/2 oz cooked rice

◆ Slice through the pork chops horizontally from one end, leaving a border on two sides to form a pocket.

◆ Cook the butter on high for 1 minute, add the onion and mushrooms and cook on high for 3 minutes. Stir in the rice.

◆ Spoon the stuffing mixture into the pockets in the pork chops and secure with wooden cocktail sticks.

◆ Arrange the chops in a dish with the thickest parts to the outer edge. Cover and cook on high for 5 minutes. Rearrange and turn the chops, then continue to cook them for a further 9–10 minutes on medium. One minute before the end of the cooking time sprinkle with the grated cheese, to melt it, or brown under a conventional grill (broiler).

◆ Serve with mushrooms and tomatoes.

PORK CHOPS WITH CRANBERRY SAUCE

SERVES 4 / SET: HIGH AND MEDIUM

Ingredients

4 loin pork chops, 150 g/6 oz each
100 g/4 oz cranberry sauce
15 ml/1 tbsp cooking oil
²/₃ cup/150 ml/¼ pint dry sherry

◆ Preheat a browning dish to the maximum recommended by the manufacturer. Press the chops onto the dish to sear, turn over and cook on high for 5 minutes.
◆ Combine the remaining ingredients and cook on high for 2 minutes. Blend to a smooth sauce and pour over the chops. Cover and cook on medium for 10–12 minutes, turning once.

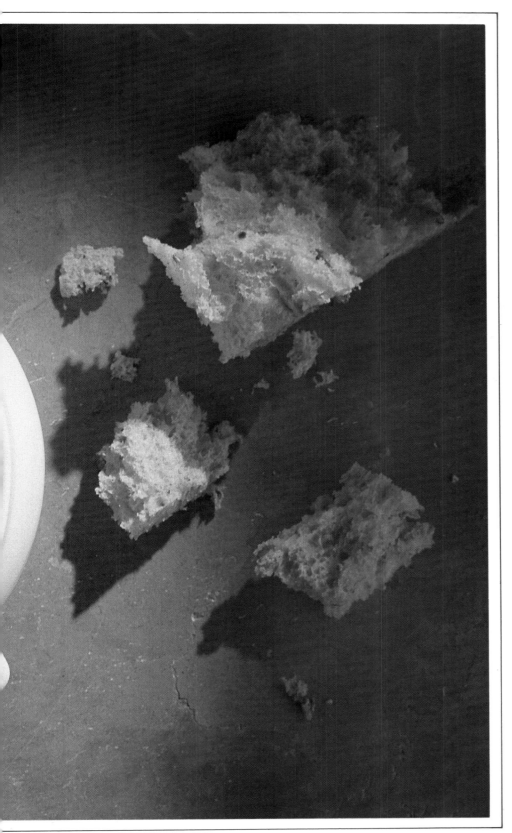

QUICK HAM AND BEAN HASH

SERVES 4—6 / SET: HIGH AND MEDIUM

Ingredients

2 tbsp/25 g/1 oz butter
4 rashers (slices) streaky (fat) bacon, diced
1 onion, chopped
400 g/14 oz can of new potatoes, diced
400 g/14 oz can of kidney beans, drained
325 g/11½ oz can of sweetcorn, drained
225 g/8 oz cooked ham, sliced
400 g/14 oz can of tomatoes, finely chopped
30 ml/2 tbsp tomato purée (paste)
15 ml/1 tbsp Worcestershire sauce
15 ml/1 tbsp soy sauce
Tabasco sauce to taste
salt and pepper to taste

◆ Place the butter, onion and bacon in a casserole, cover and cook on high for 3 minutes. Add all the remaining ingredients, stir well and heat on medium for 10–12 minutes or until piping hot.

◆ Serve with crusty bread.

Quick ham & bean hash

GLAZED BACON (HAM) ROAST

SERVES 6—8 / SET: HIGH AND MEDIUM

Ingredients

1 1/2 kg/3 lb middle gammon joint (ham roast), rind removed, soaked overnight
1/2 cup/150 ml/5 fl oz water
1/2 cup/150 ml/5 fl oz pineapple juice
3 tbsp/75 g/3 oz brown sugar
1 tbsp/15 g/1/2 oz butter

◆ Place the joint (roast) in a roasting bag with 150 ml/5 fl oz of water, pierce the bag and close it with a non metallic tie. Stand it in a dish and cook for 6 minutes on high. Reduce to medium and cook for a further 25 minutes, turning over after 12 minutes.

◆ Remove the joint from the bag and wrap it loosely in foil, shiny side inwards. Let it stand for 15 minutes.

◆ Place the pineapple juice, sugar and butter in a bowl. Cook on high for 6 minutes, stirring every 2 minutes, to make a glaze.

◆ Stand the joint in a grill (broiling) pan, brush with the glaze and brown it under a preheated conventional grill (broiler).

GAMMON HAM RISOTTO

SERVES 4 / SET: HIGH

Ingredients

2 cups/350 g/12 oz rice
2½ cups/650 ml/23 fl oz hot chicken stock (broth)
100 g/4 oz button mushrooms, sliced
1 small red pepper, chopped
100 g/4 oz frozen peas, defrosted
325 g/11 oz can sweetcorn
350 g/12 oz gammon steak (ham steak), diced
1 clove garlic, crushed
salt and pepper to taste

◆ Cook the rice in the stock for 15 minutes. Let it stand, covered, for 7 minutes.

◆ Meanwhile, place all the remaining ingredients in a dish, cover and cook for 7–9 minutes. Stir twice during the cooking time.

◆ Mix into the rice and serve.

Gammon ham risotto

HAWAIIAN GAMMON HAM

SERVES 4 / SET: HIGH

Ingredients
4 gammon (ham) slices
4 canned pineapple rings, drained
2 tbsp/25 g/1 oz butter
30 ml/2 tbsp sultanas (golden raisins)
4 slices of cheese

◆ Remove the rind from the gammon (ham) and snip the fat with scissors at regular intervals.

◆ Place the butter in a bowl, add the sultanas (golden raisins) and cook for 1½ minutes, or until they are plump and juicy.

◆ Place the gammon steak on a large plate, cover with absorbent paper and cook for 9 to 10 minutes, turning once.

◆ Remove the paper. Place one pineapple ring on each steak, fill the centre with sultanas and place a cheese slice on top. Return to the oven and cook for 2–3 minutes. Serve with tomatoes and mushrooms.

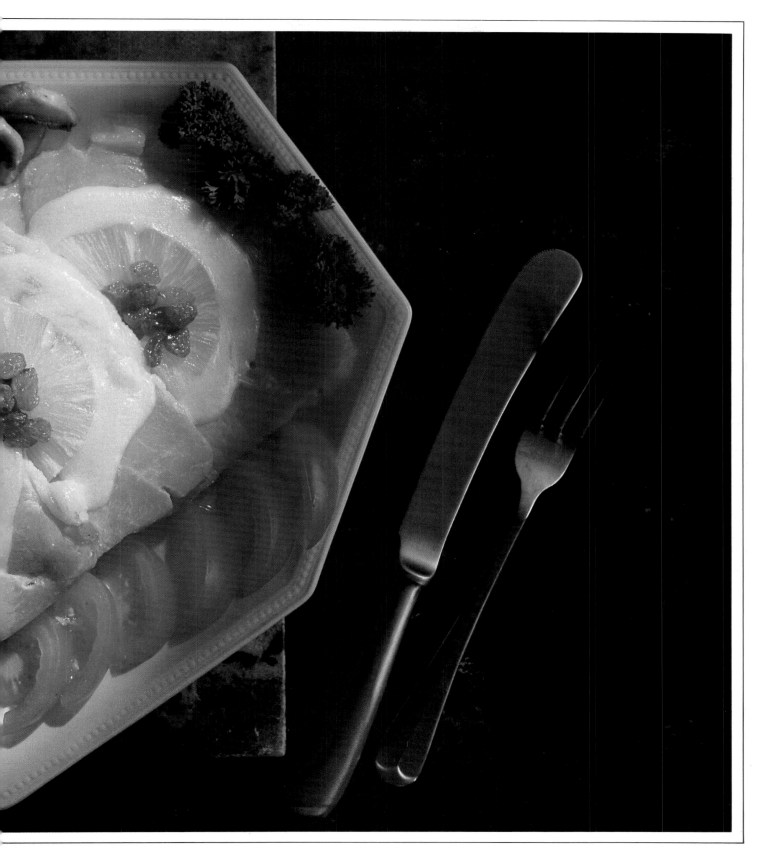

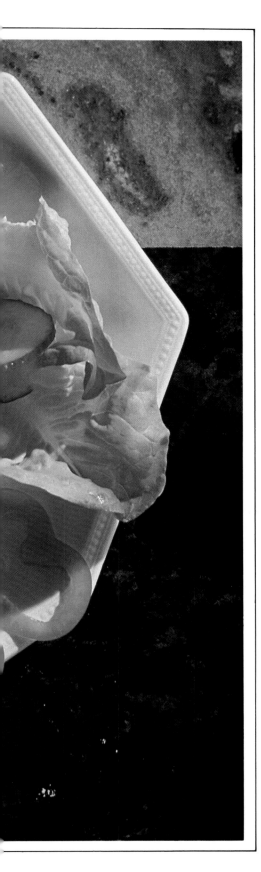

TANDOORI CHICKEN

SERVES 4 / SET: HIGH AND MEDIUM

Ingredients

4 chicken leg portions, 220 g/8 oz each

45 ml/3 tbsp tandoori or curry paste

150 ml/5 fl oz plain yoghurt

lemon wedges and onion rings to garnish

◆ Skin the chicken portions and make 3–4 deep slashes in the flesh. Place in a dish.

◆ Mix together the tandoori or curry paste and yoghurt, pour the mixture over the chicken and marinate for at least 2 hours.

◆ Remove the chicken from the marinade, place on a roasting rack, cover with the lid and cook on high for 10 minutes, turning halfway through the cooking time. Reset the oven to medium and cook for a further 15–17 minutes, turning and rearranging twice.

◆ Pierce the chicken at the joint and ensure that the juices run clear. If they are pink, return it to the oven and cook a little longer, checking regularly for doneness.

◆ Place on a grill (broiler) rack and char under a preheated conventional grill (broiler) for 5 minutes.

◆ Garnish and serve with salad and rice.

ROAST TURKEY

SERVES 2 / SET: MEDIUM

Ingredients

2 kg/4½ lb turkey

4 sticks of celery, sliced

2 small onions, quartered

2 bay leaves

2 tbsp/25 g/1 oz butter

3 slices streaky (fat) bacon

◆ Stuff the turkey with the celery, onion, bay leaves and butter.

◆ Place the turkey breast down on a roasting rack and cover with the lid. Cook for 25 minutes.

◆ Turn the bird over, lay the bacon over the breast and cook for a further 25 minutes.

◆ Discard the bacon and wrap the turkey loosely in foil. Let it stand for 10 minutes.

◆ Place turkey in a grill (broiler) pan and brown under a preheated conventional grill (broiler).

◆ Serve with roast potatoes and fresh vegetables.

Tandoori chicken

CHICKEN AND ALMONDS CHINESE STYLE

SERVES 4 / SET: HIGH

Ingredients

675 g/1½ lb boned chicken breasts, cut into thin strips

1 large onion, quartered and finely sliced

2 tbsp/50 g/2 oz blanched almonds

30 ml/2 tbsp sesame oil

1¼ cups/300 ml/½ pint chicken stock

15 ml/1 tbsp soy sauce

15 ml/1 tbsp cornflour (cornstarch) mixed with 2 teaspoons water

175 g/6 oz beansprouts

1 small sweet red pepper cut into julienne strips

1 small sweet green pepper cut into julienne strips

◆ Preheat a browning dish to the maximum recommended by the manufacturer.

◆ Add the oil to the dish with the strips of chicken and cook for 3 minutes.

◆ Add the onion and almonds. Cook for 3 minutes, stirring once during the cooking time.

◆ Blend together the chicken stock broth, soy sauce and cornflour. Stir into the chicken mixture, cover and cook for 4–5 minutes. Let it stand for 5 minutes.

◆ Place the beansprouts and the red and green peppers in a dish with 15 ml/1 tbsp water, cover with cling film (plastic wrap) and cook for 1 minute.

◆ Place the vegetables in a dish and pile the chicken and almonds on them. Serve with rice.

Chicken & almonds Chinese style

WHOLE ROAST CHICKEN

SERVES 4—6 / SET: MEDIUM

Ingredients

1.5 kg/3 lb roasting chicken

30 ml/2 tbsp clear honey

15 ml/1 tbsp soya sauce

5 ml/1 tsp paprika

2 tbsp/25 g/1 oz melted butter

◆ Mix together the honey, soya sauce and paprika. Brush the chicken with the sauce. Protect the wing tips and drumsticks with foil.

◆ Place the chicken, breast down, on a roasting rack and cover with the lid or a pierced roasting bag closed with a non-metallic tie.

◆ Calculate the cooking time at 9 minutes per pound. Halfway through, turn the chicken breast up and brush with butter. Protect the breast bone with a strip of foil. Drain off any accumulated juices from the dish and cook for the remainder of the calculated cooking time.

◆ With a sharp knife, pierce the inside thigh joint and check that the juices run clear. If they are pink, return the chicken to the oven and cook a little longer, checking at regular intervals.

◆ When completely cooked, remove from the roasting rack and cover lightly with foil. Let it stand for 15 minutes.

DUCK IN ORANGE SAUCE

SERVES 4 / SET: MEDIUM AND HIGH

Ingredients

4 duck portions, total weight approx 2 kg/4¹/₂ lb

S A U C E

15 ml/1 tbsp clear marmalade

1 cup/225 ml/8 fl oz orange juice

30 ml/2 tbsp port wine

30 ml/2 tbsp lemon juice

30 ml/2 tbsp honey

10 ml/2 tsp cornflour (cornstarch) mixed with 1 tsp water

orange slices and watercress to garnish

◆ Arrange the duck portions on a rack in a large deep dish. Cook covered on medium for 45–60 minutes. Reposition and turn the pieces over several times during the cooking period and drain off the surplus fat. Test to see that they are cooked by piercing with a sharp knife at the joint, the juices should run clear. Brown the cooked duck under a conventional grill (broiler).

◆ For the sauce, place the marmalade jelly in a dish and cook on high for 1 minute. Add the rest of the sauce ingredients and cook for a further 3 minutes or until bubbling. Cool slightly and stir in the cornflour, cook on high for 1 minute and stir well.

◆ Place the duck on a warm serving dish, pour over the sauce and garnish with orange slices and watercress.

CHICKEN MARENGO

S E R V E S   4   /   S E T :   H I G H
A N D   M E D I U M

Ingredients

1 onion, finely chopped
4 chicken portions approx 227 g/8 oz each
400 g/14 oz can of tomatoes
225 g/8 oz button mushrooms
2 celery sticks, sliced
10 ml/2 tsp celery salt
45 ml/3 tbsp tomato purée (paste)
1 clove garlic, crushed
5 ml/1 tsp mixed dried herbs
2 tbsp/25 g/1 oz butter, diced
2 tbsp/25 g/1 oz flour
½ cup/150 ml/¼ pint hot chicken stock (broth)
½ cup/150 ml/¼ pint red wine
salt and pepper to taste
onion rings to garnish

◆ Place the onion in a casserole dish, cover and cook on high for 2 minutes. Add the chicken portions, thick parts to the outer edge of the dish, cover and cook on high for 6 minutes. Keep to one side.

◆ Place tomatoes, mushrooms, celery, celery salt, tomato purée (paste), garlic and herbs in a bowl. Cover and cook on high for 3 minutes, stirring once during the cooking time.

◆ Stir in the butter until melted, add flour, chicken stock and wine. Cover and cook on high for 4 minutes, stirring after 2 minutes.

◆ Add the sauce to the casserole and cook covered on medium for 30–35 minutes. Let it stand for 5 minutes.

◆ Season to taste, garnish and serve.

Chicken Marengo

BRAISED PIGEONS

SERVES 4 / SET: HIGH

Ingredients

4 pigeons or Cornish hens, total weight
1.25 kg/2½ lb

STUFFING

1 large onion, quartered and finely
chopped

2 sticks of celery, sliced

2 bay leaves

50 g/2 oz mushrooms, sliced

SAUCE

10 ml/2 tsp mixed dried herbs

2 tbsp/25 g/1 oz butter, diced

2 tbsp/25 g/1 oz flour

100 g/4 oz button mushrooms, sliced

1¼ cups/300 ml/½ pint hot chicken stock

1¼ cups/300 ml/½ pint red wine

ground black pepper

◆ Combine the stuffing ingredients
and stuff the pigeons.

◆ Place the birds in a casserole dish,
breast down. Cover and cook for 10
minutes. Turn pigeons over the cook
uncovered for 6½ minutes. Set aside,
covered.

◆ Cook the butter for 1 minute then
add the flour and mushrooms. Cook
for a further 1 minute. Stir in the
stock, wine and pepper to taste. Cook
uncovered for 5 minutes, stirring
every minute.

◆ Pour the sauce over the pigeons,
cover and cook for 7½ minutes. Let it
stand covered for 5 minutes.

QUICK CHICKEN PASTA

SERVES 4 / SET: HIGH

Ingredients

350 g/12 oz green tagliatelle
15 ml/1 tbsp cooking oil
5 ml/1 tsp salt
1 small red pepper, diced
1 small green pepper, diced
100 g/4 oz frozen peas, defrosted
295-g/10½-oz can of condensed mushroom soup
½ cup/150 ml/5 fl oz water
450 g/1 lb cooked chicken, diced

◆ Place pasta in a deep dish and pour over enough boiling water to cover. Add the oil and salt, cover and cook for 6 minutes. Let it stand for 6 minutes.

◆ Place the peppers in a dish, cover and cook for 3 minutes. Add the peas and cook for a further 3 minutes.

◆ Combine the mushroom soup and water, and add it with the chicken to the vegetables. Cook uncovered for 6–8 minutes, stirring once halfway through the cooking time.

◆ Drain the pasta and place in a warm serving dish. Arrange the chicken mixture on top and serve.

TURKEY BREASTS CORDON BLEU

SERVES 4 / SET: HIGH & LOW

Ingredients

4 turkey breasts, approx 150 g/6 oz each
¼ cup/50 g/2 oz butter, diced
4 slices of ham
4 slices of mozzarella cheese
pinch of paprika

◆ Place the turkey breasts in a shallow dish and dot with the butter. Cover and cook on high for 4 minutes. Rearrange and turn the breasts over, cover and cook on low for 5–6 minutes, turning them again half way through the cooking time.

◆ Transfer the pieces to a microwave proof serving dish. Place a slice of ham and a slice of cheese on top of each breast and cook on high, uncovered, for 3 minutes.

◆ Sprinkle with paprika and serve.

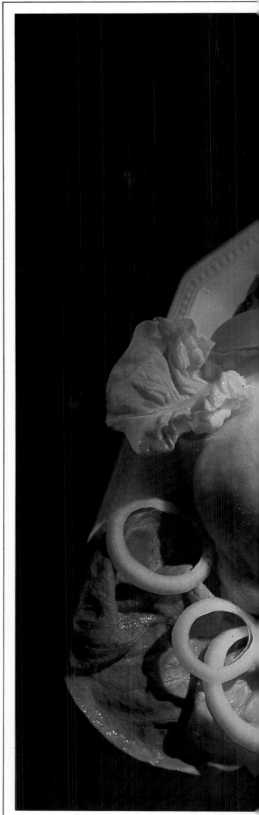

Turkey breasts Cordon Bleu

ROAST POUSSINS (CORNISH GAME HENS)

S E R V E S   2 / S E T :   M E D I U M

Ingredients

2 oven ready poussins (Cornish game hens), 500 g/1 lb each

S T U F F I N G

150 g/5 oz redcurrant jelly

3 tbsp/40 g/1½ oz butter

3 tbsp/50 g/2 oz cooked rice

30 ml/2 tbsp sultanas (golden raisins)

salt and pepper to taste

G L A Z E

30 ml/2 tbsp soya sauce

15 ml/1 tbsp honey

◆ Combine the stuffing ingredients in a bowl, cover and cook for 1½ minutes.

◆ Stuff the poussins and lay them on a roasting rack, breast down.

◆ Mix the soya sauce and honey in a bowl, and cook for 1 minute. Brush the poussins with half the glaze, cover with a lid and cook for 15 minutes.

◆ Drain, then turn the poussins breast up. Coat with the remainder of the glaze, cover and cook for a further 15 minutes. Remove from rack, cover in foil and allow to stand for 10 minutes.

Roast poussins

LIVER AND BACON KEBABS

S E R V E S   2 / S E T :   H I G H

Ingredients

225 g/8 oz chicken livers

8 slices streaky bacon

100 g/4 oz button mushrooms

Worcestershire sauce to taste

◆ Cut each bacon slice into 2 or 3 pieces and wrap the pieces around the livers.

◆ Skewer them onto wooden kebab sticks, alternating with the mushrooms. Sprinkle with Worcestershire sauce to taste.

◆ Place the kebabs on a plate in an even layer. Cover with absorbent paper and cook for 6–7 minutes, turning once during the cooking time.

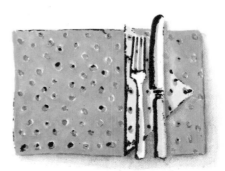

VEAL ITALIENNE

*SERVES 4 / SET: HIGH
AND MEDIUM*

Ingredients

350 g/12 oz tagliatelle
5 ml/1 tsp oil
5 ml/1 tsp salt
450 g/1 lb diced fillet of veal
220 g/8 oz diced gammon (ham) steak
1 tbsp/14 g/1/2 oz butter
1 large onion, thinly sliced
100 g/4 oz button mushrooms, halved
2 gherkins (pickles), chopped

SAUCE

2 tbsp/25 g/1 oz butter
2 tbsp/25 g/1 oz flour
1 1/4 cups/250 ml/1/2 pint milk
salt and pepper to taste
julienne strips of sweet red pepper to garnish

◆ Place the pasta in a deep dish, pour over enough boiling water to cover, add the salt and 5 ml/1 tsp of oil. Cook on high for 6 minutes. Cover and keep to one side.

◆ Place the veal, gammon (ham) and butter in a dish. Cover and cook on high for 3 minutes, stirring once. Add the onion and mushrooms. Cook on high for 2 minutes and place to one side.

◆ For the sauce, melt the butter on high for 1 minute then stir in the flour and cook for a further minute. Add the milk and cook on high for 3 minutes, stirring every minute. Add this to the meat mixture and cook on medium for 15 minutes. Stir in the chopped gherkins (pickles) and season to taste.

◆ Drain the pasta, arrange in a serving dish and top with the meat sauce. Garnish and serve.

VEAL ROULADE AND MUSHROOM SAUCE

*S E R V E S   4   /   S E T :   H I G H
A N D   M E D I U M*

Ingredients

4 veal escalopes (fillets) beaten thin

2 large carrots cut into long sticks

30 ml/2 tbsp water

8 frozen French (green) beans

4 tbsp/50 g/2 oz butter

S A U C E

295 g/10 oz can condensed mushroom soup

½ cup/150 ml/5 fl oz water

salt and pepper to taste

◆ Cook the carrots in 2 tbsp of water in a covered dish for 3 minutes on high. Add the French (green) beans and cook for 1 minute.

◆ Lay the escalopes (veal fillets) on a board and place a carrot stick and 2 beans at the shortest end. Roll up neatly and secure each roll with a wooden cocktail stick.

◆ Arrange the veal in a shallow dish, dot with butter, cover and cook for 5 minutes on high. Rearrange and continue to cook for a further 9 minutes on medium. Add salt and pepper to taste, cover and reserve.

◆ Blend the soup with the water and cook on high for 5 minutes or until hot. Transfer to a warm sauceboat.

◆ Remove cocktail sticks from roulades and slice into even-sized rings. Serve with the sauce, new potatoes, French (green) beans and carrots.

MEAT AND FRUIT PILAFF

SERVES 4 / SET: HIGH AND MEDIUM

Ingredients

350 g/12 oz brown rice
650 ml/12 fl oz hot chicken stock (broth)
225 g/8 oz diced cooked meat
1 banana, sliced
1 red apple, diced
1 green apple, diced
1 peach, peeled and diced
15 ml/1 tbsp lemon juice
100 g/4 oz cashew nuts
50 g/2 oz sultanas (golden raisins)
salt and pepper to taste

◆ Place the rice in a deep dish, add the hot stock, cover and cook on high for 30–35 minutes. Let it stand, covered, for 10 minutes.

◆ Toss the apples and banana in the lemon juice. Combine with the rest of the ingredients. Cover and cook on medium for 5 minutes. Mix into the cooked rice and serve.

FRESH VEGETABLES/COOKING GUIDE

vegetables	quantity	minutes on full
globe artichokes	4	10 – 20
asparagus spears	1½ cups/225 g/8 oz	6 – 7
aubergines (eggplant), diced	2 cups/450 g/1 lb	5 – 6
beans, broad (fava, lima), French (green) or runner	2½ cups/450 g/1 lb	8 – 10
beetroot (beets), sliced	4 cups/450 g/1 lb	7 – 8
broccoli florets	6 cups/450 g/1 lb	4 – 5
Brussels sprouts	6 cups/450 g/1 lb	8 – 10
cabbage, shredded	6 cups/450 g/1 lb	7 – 10
carrots, sliced	2 cups/225 g/8 oz	7 – 10
cauliflower florets	6 cups/450 g/1 lb	10 – 11
celery	1 head	10 – 13
corn on the cob	1	3 – 5
courgettes (zucchini), sliced	4	7 – 10
Kohlraki	4 cups/450 g/1 lb	7 – 8
leeks, sliced	4 cups/450 g/1 lb	7 – 10
marrow (squash), sliced	4 cups/450 g/1 lb	8 – 10
mushrooms, whole	2½ cups/225 g/8 oz	5 – 6
okra	4 cups/450 g/1 lb	8 – 10
onions, sliced	2 cups/225 g/8 oz	5 – 7
parsnips, sliced	2 cups/225 g/8 oz	8 – 10
peas	4 cups/450 g/1 lb	7
potatoes, new	6 cups/450 g/1 lb	8 – 10
potatoes, jacket (baked)	2 large	8
potatoes, boiled	4 cups/450 g/1 lb	6 – 7
spinach	2 cups/450 g/1 lb	5
greens, chopped	6 cups/450 g/1 lb	7 – 9
swedes (rutabaga), sliced	3 cups/450 g/1 lb	6 – 7
tomatoes, sliced	1½ cups/450 g/1 lb	2 – 3
turnips, sliced	1½ cups/225 g/8 oz	6 – 7

FROZEN VEGETABLES/COOKING GUIDE

vegetables	quantity	minutes on full
asparagus spears	1½ cups/225 g/8 oz	6 – 7
beans, broad (fava), French (green) or runner	1½ cups/225 g/8 oz	7
broccoli spears	4 cups/225 g/8 oz	6 – 8
cabbage, chopped	3 cups/225 g/8 oz	6 – 7
carrots, sliced	2 cups/225 g/8 oz	6 – 7
cauliflower florets	4 cups/225 g/8 oz	4 – 6
sweetcorn (corn)	2 cups/225 g/8 oz	4 – 6
corn on the cob	1	4 – 5
courgettes (zucchini), sliced	2 cups/225 g/8 oz	4
peas	2 cups/225 g/8 oz	4
spinach, chopped	3 cups/225 g/8 oz	5
swedes (rutabaga), cubed	2 cups/225 g/8 oz	7
turnips, sliced	1½ cups/225 g/8 oz	8
vegetables, mixed	2 cups/225 g/8 oz	4 – 6

FRESH MEAT COOKING GUIDE

meat	minutes on full per 450 g/1 lb	standing minutes
bacon (ham) roast	12 – 14	10
bacon, rashers (slices) 4	4½	—
beef, boned roasts, rare	5 – 6	15 – 20
beef, boneless roast, medium	7 – 8	15 – 20
beef, boneless roast, well-done	8 – 9	15 – 20
beef, roasts with bone, rare	5 – 6	15 – 20
beef, roasts with bone, medium	6 – 7	15 – 20
beef, roasts with bone, well-done	8 – 9	15 – 20
beef, ground, 4 patties	10	5
chicken, whole roast	8 – 10	10 – 15
chicken, portions	6 – 8	10
lamb, boned roast	7 – 8	20
lamb, boned and rolled roast	9	20
lamb, roast with bone	6 – 7	20
lamb, crown roast	9 – 10	20
lamb chops	2	10
liver, ox (beef)	8	5
liver, lamb, calves'	7	5
pork, boned rolled roast	8 – 10	15
pork, roast with bone	8 – 9	15
poussin (Cornish rock hen), pigeon, pheasant, quail	5 – 7	5
sausages (links), 4	4	—
portions	15	10
turkey, whole roast	11	10 – 15

FROZEN MEAT DEFROSTING GUIDE

meat	minutes on low per 450 g/1 lb	standing minutes
beef, boned roasts	8 – 10	30
beef, roasts on bone	8 – 10	30
beef, minced (ground)	8 – 10	2
beef steak, cubed	6 – 8	5
hamburgers, two	2	2
hamburgers, four	4	2
chicken, whole	6 – 8	30
chicken portions	5	30
duck and duckling	5 – 7	30
kidney	6 – 9	5
lamb, boned roasts	5 – 6	30 – 45
lamb, with bone	8 – 10	30 – 45
lamb chops	8 – 10	15
liver	8 – 10	5
pork, boned roasts	7 – 8	30
pork roast with bone	7 – 8	45
poussin (Cornish rock hen), grouse, pigeon, pheasant	5 – 7	10
sausages (links)	5 – 6	5
turkey, whole	10 – 12	60
veal, boned rolled roast	5 – 6	30
veal, with bone	8 – 10	45
veal chops	8 – 10	30
veal, minced (ground)	8 – 10	5

FISH
Defrost and Cooking Guide

fish	weight	defrost minutes	standing minutes	cooking in minutes on full
bass	225 g/8 oz	5 – 6	15	5 – 6
bonito tuna steaks,	225 g/8 oz	10	15	—
bream, sea-bream	225 g/8 oz	—	15	10 – 12
cod fillets	225 g/8 oz	4 – 5	5	4 – 6
cod steaks	225 g/8 oz	5	5	6
crab claws	100 g/4 oz	5	5	2 – 3
crab, dressed (crab cakes)	100 g/4 oz	2	10	—
haddock fillets	100 g/4 oz	4 – 5	5	5 – 7
haddock steaks	100 g/4 oz	4 – 5	5	4 – 7
halibut steaks	100 g/4 oz	4 – 5	5	4 – 5
hake steaks	100 g/4 oz	4 – 5	5	4 – 6
kipper (kippered herrings)	100 g/4 oz	—	—	1 – 2
kipper (kippered herrings) fillets (boil-in-the-bag)	200 g/7 oz	3	5	3
mackerel	225 g/8 oz	6 – 8	8 – 10	4 – 5
mahi-mahi	225 g/8 oz	6 – 8	—	4 – 6
red and grey mullet	225 g/8 oz	6 – 8	8 – 10	4 – 6
mussels	225 g/8 oz	5	5	—
plaice (flounder) fillets	225 g/8 oz	4 – 5	5	4
prawns (small shrimp), cooked	225 g/8 oz	5	5	—
red salmon steaks	225 g/8 oz	5	5	4 – 5
scrod fillets	225 g/8 oz	4 – 5	30	4 – 5
scampi (king prawns), raw		5	5	4 – 6
scallops	225 g/8 oz	5	5	5 – 7
snapper	225 g/8 oz	6 – 8	8 – 10	5 – 7
sole	225 g/8 oz	5 – 6	8 – 10	4
trout	225 g/8 oz	6 – 8	8 – 10	7
yellowtail	225 g/8 oz	6 – 8	8 – 10	7

TIME AND SETTINGS FOR PASTA AND GRAINS

Although there are no real time savings in cooking rice and pasta in the microwave, it may be a more foolproof way of cooking as there is no risk of sticking to the pan. Standing is usually necessary to complete cooking.

Cooking times will vary according to the type of pasta. Fresh pasta needs microwaving for only 1 minute. It requires no standing time, but should just be drained and served immediately. Times for dried pasta and rice are given below.

PASTA AND GRAINS COOKING GUIDE
PER 225 G/8 OZ

food	boiling salted water to add	cooking in minutes on full	standing minutes
long grain rice (1 generous cup)	3 cups/725 ml/1¼ pt	14	5
pudding (Carolina) rice (1 generous cup)	2½ cups/600 ml/1 pt		
American (converted) rice (2½ cups)	2½ cups/600 ml/ 1 pint	12	5
brown rice	3½ cups/900 ml/ 1½ pt	30	5
egg noodles & tagliatelle (fettucini) (6 cups)	4 cups/1 litre/1¾ pt with 2 tsp oil	6 – 8	2 – 3
spaghetti	4 cups/1 litre/1¾ pt with 2 tsp oil	12	5 – 10
pasta shells (2 cups) & shapes	4 cups/1 litre/1¾ pt with 2 tsp oil	12 – 14	5 – 10
macaroni (2 cups)	4 cups/1 litre/1¾ pt with 2 tsp oil	12 – 15	2 – 3
lasagne (6 cups)	4 cups/1 litre/1¾ pt with 2 tsp oil	9	2

CAKES, BREAD AND DESSERTS DEFROSTING GUIDE

product	quantity	minutes on low	standing minutes
bread, whole loaf	1 large	6 – 8	5 – 15
bread, whole loaf	1 small	4 – 6	10
bread, sliced loaf	1 large	6 – 8	10
bread, sliced loaf	1 small	4 – 6	5
bread slice	25 g/1 oz	10 – 15 secs	1 – 2
bread rolls, crumpets,	2	15 – 20 secs	1 – 2
scones (biscuits), etc	4	25 – 35	1 – 2
cakes, cream	2	45 – 60	10
	4	1¼	10
cakes, small	2	30 – 60	5
cupcakes	4	1¼ – 1¾	5
cakes, large: sponge (yellow) cake	450 g/1 lb	4	10
cheesecake	23 cm/9 in	3 – 4	20
dough, pizza and bread	450 g/1 lb	4	10
dough, shortcrust and puff	227 g/8 oz	4	20
dough, shortcrust and puff	397 g/14 oz	6	20
mousse (soufflé), small	1	30 secs	15
pie, fruit or cream	650 g/26 oz	5	10
trifle	1	1	15